Hegl

21st
Century
Skills Library

COOL CAREERS

MULTIMEDIA ARTIST AND ANIMATOR

MATT MULLINS

Published in the United States of America by
Cherry Lake Publishing, Ann Arbor, Michigan
www.cherrylakepublishing.com

Content Adviser
Terrence Masson, BFA, MFA, Director of Creative Industries, Northeastern University

Credits
Photos: Cover and page 1, ©Picture Contact/Alamy; page 4, ©emin kuliyev/
Shutterstock, Inc.; pages 5, 18, and 27, ©iStockphoto.com/track5; page 7,
©David Calicchio/Dreamstime.com; page 10, ©iStockphoto.com/mumininan;
page 12, ©iStockphoto.com/Maica; page 15, ©Leah-Anne Thompson/Shutterstock,
Inc.; page 17, ©Laylandmasuda/Dreamstime.com; page 20, ©Jacek Chabraszewski/
Shutterstock, Inc.; page 21, ©BarracudaDesigns/Shutterstock, Inc.; page 23,
©Paul Clarke/Shutterstock, Inc.; page 24, ©iStockphoto.com/kryczka; page 26,
©iStockphoto.com/gecko753

Library of Congress Cataloging-in-Publication Data
Mullins, Matt.
  Multimedia artist and animator/by Matt Mullins.
     p. cm.—(Cool careers)
  Includes bibliographical references and index.
  ISBN-13: 978-1-60279-942-4 (lib. bdg.)
  ISBN-10: 1-60279-942-3 (lib. bdg.)
 1. Commercial art—Vocational guidance—Juvenile literature.
 2. Commercial artists—Vocational guidance—Juvenile literature.
 3. Animators—Vocational guidance—Juvenile literature. I. Title. II. Series.
  NC1001.M85 2010
  741.5'8023—dc22   2010002823

Cherry Lake Publishing would like to acknowledge
the work of The Partnership for 21st Century Skills.
Please visit www.21stcenturyskills.org for more information.

Printed in the United States of America
Corporate Graphics Inc.
July 2010
CLFA07

TABLE OF CONTENTS

CHAPTER ONE

MULTIMEDIA ART AND ANIMATION IS EVERYWHERE

Have you ever been in a big city? You probably saw pictures and drawings everywhere. Banners at bus stops.

In New York City's Times Square, advertisements cover the sides of almost every building.

Billboards. Giant television screens. Logos on buildings and in windows.

Think about being home. What art do you see at home? What shows do you watch on television? What art have you made yourself?

Art is all around us. Some of it is for entertainment. Some of it tries to convince you to buy things. Some tries to convince you to go places.

It comes in many **media**, including paintings, advertisements, sculptures, **animation**, and **art installations**. It is on your computer. When you start up the computer, you often see a logo. An artist created that logo. When you see a poster in your classroom, you're seeing something made by an artist. At a Web site, you see art and designs. Some are animated, like moving cartoons. Others remain still, like a photograph. Even the Web site itself has been designed. Designers arrange words, pictures, and drawings in ways that make the site fun and interesting to look at.

There are many, many multimedia artists and animators who create the **images** and designs you see every day.

It is an exciting career that offers many opportunities for work. You can work in advertising. You can work as a multimedia artist in film or television. You can work on video games. The multimedia artists and animators who do this work have interesting, exciting jobs.

LEARNING & INNOVATION SKILLS

Multimedia artists do a wide variety of jobs. They design the words and images on your cereal box. They also create the interactive features on your favorite Web sites. These let you click on something to open a video or jump to another Web site.

What ties all this together? Communication. Multimedia artists and animators help people communicate visually. Companies who sell things want people to buy their products. Organizations want people to be interested in their work. What ways do you see people or companies using images to communicate? What do you think they are trying to communicate?

Multimedia artists need to think carefully about how audiences will react to their work.

CHAPTER TWO
A DAY ON THE JOB

The Multimedia Artist

Maciej is a **commercial** multimedia artist. He works for a biotechnology company. Maciej prepares advertising and art of many kinds, including scientific illustrations.

Multimedia artists and animators sometimes work together in busy offices.

Maciej goes to work on a Monday morning. The first task of the day is a meeting of designers. They talk about the work they have ahead for the week. They talk about the work to do that day. The meeting lasts 30 minutes and ends on time.

Then Maciej heads to his desk to work. He reviews a stack of requests. Sometimes he's asked to design a brochure about a company product. He might have to work on a sign for a trade show, where his company will display the product. There are also times when he has to correct something. But his favorite task is to illustrate scientific processes and figures.

Maciej loves scientific illustrations. He may be asked to show a part of a cell or how molecules interact. He starts with pen and paper. He begins sketching. Sometimes he draws more than one version on a sheet. Sometimes he draws a very detailed picture. Other times it's a rough sketch that gives a basic idea of what he's working on.

When he has something he likes, he takes a picture of it. Then he connects his digital camera to his computer. He loads the picture onto his computer. Then he takes the image and puts it into an illustration program. Maciej builds on the sketched image. He sharpens lines. He adds shading. He makes sure parts connect or point to other parts in the right way.

When he's happy with his image, he sends it to an art director. The art director sends it on to the people who asked for the art. Many times, these people have suggestions about changes to the image. Sometimes the art director has suggestions. Maciej considers all the ideas and works more on his drawing.

Maciej works closely with others. The drawing has been reviewed by a number of people by the time it is done.

Multimedia artists and animators must be able to listen to advice and criticism from others.

The Artist

Melissa is an artist and an illustrator. She works in a studio. Her studio has drawing, painting, and sculpting supplies. Melissa works on many kinds of projects. She creates art for graphic novels or comic books. She paints. She works on images for posters or other advertisements.

LIFE & CAREER SKILLS

Multimedia artists and animators may do their work alone, but the work is always done with someone else's input. Supervisors, customers, or even coworkers review the work and give feedback. Sometimes they want little things changed. Sometimes they want something totally different. Changes may get asked for again and again.

To work as a multimedia artist and animator, you must have a thick skin. At some point, someone may say, "That's not really what we're looking for." An artist has to be **professional** about accepting criticism. Sometimes after all these changes, something new or unexpected is created!

Usually her day starts with coffee. She arrives at her studio and turns on some music. She then sketches an object she wants to sculpt or an art installation she wants to create. If she has a sculpture she's not sure about, she'll take it apart. She'll put it together in a new way.

When she's illustrating, she works one, two, or three hours at a time. Melissa finds it hard to sit still! She also works as

Some artists choose to work in comfortable studios that help them feel creative.

a volunteer art teacher for children and adults. She loves to teach painting and sculpture.

Melissa's work keeps her busy. It's always interesting.

The Animator

Peter worked for seven seasons on the Comedy Central show *South Park*. An animated program for adults, *South Park* is very popular. It looks like paper animation. The characters and **sets** look cut out from colored art paper. But everything is made using computer programs. *Animate* means "bring life to." By moving the shapes in just the right way, Peter made the characters come to life.

Much of Peter's job involved working with story artists. Story artists would sketch parts of the show's story. Peter would **scan** these sketches into computer software. Then he would take these images and work with them. He would add color. He would also add **texture**. This would make the image look like it would feel a certain way if you touched it.

The longest day of each week for Peter was Tuesday. The program aired on Wednesday nights. On Tuesdays, Peter would come into work at 10 A.M. There would usually be one or two **scenes** left to finish. Sometimes Peter would work on one. He might put in a new background. For example, if the scene took place at a Walmart he'd create a Walmart background.

Throughout the day, the directors of the program would ask for scene changes. Maybe one character wore a blue shirt. If she was standing in front of a blue building in the scene Peter was working on, she might be hard to see. Her blue shirt would make her fade into the blue surroundings.

21ST CENTURY CONTENT

Art requires tools. For centuries, artists have used pencils, paper, paint, and canvas for drawing and painting.

Computers changed this. One example is the tablet computer. With this, designers and **graphic artists** can create all sorts of images onscreen using a pen or finger. They can erase. They can make the lines thicker or thinner, sharper or fuzzier. They can add layers over what they have drawn.

Have you ever used a computer to draw something? What did you like about this method? How do you think a computer drawing is different from a painting or pencil drawing?

Tablet computers have changed the way multimedia artists do their jobs.

Peter or another animator would adjust the colors. Maybe they would make the building darker. Maybe they'd make the girl's shirt brighter. Maybe they would change the shirt color altogether. Sometimes they'd change the texture of the "paper."

This work would go on all day. At night, some animators would go home. Peter sometimes stayed. Sometimes he would leave at 3 A.M. the next day. Other times, he might not leave until 10 A.M. the next day! The show would be on TV that night.

Animators, artists, and multimedia artists all work hard. All of them have interesting jobs. They all make great-looking art. It is hard work, but it is also very satisfying.

LIFE & CAREER SKILLS

Some jobs require working to meet deadlines. Certain tasks need to be finished by agreed upon times. Workers need to do whatever it takes to get the task completed on time. Why do you think it is important for workers to meet deadlines? What do you think might happen to a worker who doesn't meet a deadline?

It can take a long time for an artist to get a piece just the way she wants it.

CHAPTER THREE

BECOMING A MULTIMEDIA ARTIST AND ANIMATOR

There are many ways to become a multimedia artist and animator. Multimedia artists may have had graphic design

Multimedia artists and animators often go to school so they can learn to use software that will help them create their art.

training at a 2-year or 4-year college. Maciej holds a 2-year degree in graphic design.

Melissa took a different route. She received a Bachelor of Fine Arts degree. Then she studied in Italy for a year. She has done other post-college training, too. She holds a Master of Fine Arts degree now.

Peter received a Master of Fine Arts degree, too. It was a 3-year program he joined after college. Peter feels it prepared him well for the work he does now.

All of them say drawing is very important. If you love to draw, keep at it. Practice, practice, practice. Whatever schooling you decide upon, drawing will always be the best way to prepare for a career as a multimedia artist or animator.

Peter says he always carries around a pen and art paper. He draws often. Maciej says drawing a lot helps you learn how to **observe** the world around you better. Melissa agrees. She says she's always been a doodler. She feels she should doodle and draw more. She also stresses being open to anything. Melissa has painted murals for pedestrian crosswalks in New Zealand. She's painted educational murals at California health clinics. She's taught art in women's prisons.

There are many ways to prepare to become a multimedia artist and animator. The key is to keep at it. Sketch, watch things, and think about what you see. Think about what looks cool. Think about why it looks cool to you. Ask yourself what about it holds your attention. Think about how you might do it differently.

Study different kinds of art. Museums can be great places to see modern art and art that was created hundreds or even thousands of years ago. Art is about seeing things and drawing. Look at things and make things. That is how you become an artist.

It's always a good idea to practice your drawing skills.

Be creative! Try out all kinds of new ideas.

LEARNING & INNOVATION SKILLS

Multimedia artists and animators do many different kinds of work. Some are painters and sculptors. Some work on video games. Others teach at schools and universities, adult education centers, or even workplaces. Some are musicians who sing and play instruments in time with video, light shows, and other art.

Many use their skills to help others. For example, some artists work with low-income people to fix up their homes without spending much money.

The key is to do what you enjoy. Then you can find a place for art in the work you do. What ways can you imagine to combine art with other kinds of work?

Sometimes businesses hire artists to paint murals and designs on the sides of buildings.

CHAPTER FOUR
THE FUTURE FOR ART AND MULTIMEDIA

There's so much multimedia art and animation around us. New art and animation is constantly being created, and people

In the future, computers and other technology will become more important for most multimedia artists and animators.

will be needed to create more. Employment in multimedia art and animation will continue to grow, according to the U.S. government. There were about 79,000 multimedia artists and animators in the United States in 2008. By 2018, the government believes there will be more than 90,000.

There are many talented, creative people in the world. It will always be a field with a lot of competition. It will take both talent and determination to find work.

21ST CENTURY CONTENT

According to the U.S. government, half of all multimedia artists and animators earned between $41,710 and $77,010 in 2008. Those who worked in film and video earned an average of $65,600. Those in advertising earned about $52,530.

Art directors earned more. Fine artists such as painters, sculptors, and illustrators earned less. Why do you think art directors and artists in the film industry make more money?

The work will change as new technologies develop. Computer software will make some things easier. It will add new kinds of things to do. But for the most part, the role of artists and animators will stay the same.

They will continue to carefully observe the world. They will probably always have a pencil and paper close by. They will continue to practice different ways to present images.

Technology may change, but drawing will always be an important skill for artists.

Keep practicing and one day you could become a multimedia artist or animator.

They will continue to create new ways to show objects and ideas.

No matter the technology, multimedia artists and animators will still do what they've done for many years. They will communicate through images.

21ST CENTURY CONTENT

Traditional animated movies, such as *Snow White and the Seven Dwarfs* (1937) and *The Little Mermaid* (1989), are drawn on **celluloid**, a kind of plastic. Artists use a series of overlapping layers of celluloid to create moving objects on fixed backgrounds.

Now, computer graphics are much more common in animation. One example is **motion capture** animation. Director James Cameron used this in the film *Avatar* (2009). Cameron used computers to capture the movement of his actors. Then he used the recorded movement to make the blue aliens on the moon-world Pandora. When *Avatar* was released, it was the most detailed digital animation ever used in film.

SOME WELL-KNOWN MULTIMEDIA ARTISTS AND ANIMATORS

Saul Bass (1920–1996) was a true multimedia artist. He won awards for his work in film and graphic design. Bass designed logos for AT&T, United Airlines, Continental Airlines, and many other companies. He won a 1968 Academy Award as director of a documentary movie, *Why Man Creates*. Bass may be more famous for his work on movie title sequences. Title sequences show words and images at the beginning of a movie. The titles tell us who made the movie, who is in it, and more.

Hayao Miyazaki (1941–) has been making animated movies since 1971. Miyazaki first became well known in the United States in 1997 with the film *Princess Mononoke*. Miyazaki has also illustrated several graphic novels, or *manga* as they are known in Japan. His film work is in the *anime* style of Japan. Miyazaki works mostly with hand-drawn animation. He also uses some computer graphics in his films.

Nick Park (1958–) is an animator. He's probably most famous for his Wallace and Gromit movies. Park works with clay. He makes figures out of clay, then takes pictures. Park won his first of four Academy Awards for best animated short film in 1991 with *Creature Comforts*.

Leonardo da Vinci (1452–1519) may be the most famous multimedia artist. Da Vinci was a sculptor and painter, an architect and musician, a scientist, engineer, inventor, writer, and more. He may be best known as the painter of *The Last Supper* and *Mona Lisa*.

GLOSSARY

animation (an-ih-MAY-shuhn) making something look alive, such as a cartoon character

art installations (ART in-stuh-LAY-shuhnz) performances, sculptures, or other art created and shown in the same place

celluloid (SELL-yoo-loyd) a tough, plastic material used to make film for movies

commercial (kuh-MUHR-shuhl) done for the purpose of making a profit

graphic artists (GRAF-ik AHR-tistss) artists who design and make printed material, electronic art, and many other published designs

images (IM-ih-jiz) forms, appearances, or pictures of things

media (MEE-dee-uh) materials or techniques an artist uses

motion capture (MOH-shuhn CAP-chur) recording the movement of real people and using it to create computer-animated characters

observe (uhb-ZURV) to see or watch

professional (proh-FESH-uh-nuhl) doing something in a business-like way

scan (SKAN) to create a copy of an object as a computer file

scenes (SEENZ) parts of a film or show that take place at a particular time and location

sets (SEHTSS) the places or areas in which the action of a film or show is filmed

texture (TEKS-chur) the way something feels, or the look of the way it would feel

FOR MORE INFORMATION

BOOKS

Marcovitz, Hal. *Computer Animation*. Detroit: Lucent Books, 2008.

Reeves, Diane Lindsey. *Career Ideas for Kids Who Like Art*. New York: Ferguson, 2007.

Thompson, Lisa. *Art in Action: Have You Got What it Takes to Be an Animator?* Minneapolis: Compass Point Books, 2008.

WEB SITES

The Art Zone
www.nga.gov/kids/zone/zone.htm
Play games to learn about all kinds of art, from still life to 3-D animation.

Larry's Toon Institute: Lesson Plan
www.awn.com/tooninstitute/lessonplan/lesson.htm
Get lessons from Disney animator Larry Lauria on hand-drawn animation.

INDEX

ABOUT THE AUTHOR

Matt Mullins lives in Madison, Wisconsin, with his son and writes about a variety of topics for academics, consultants, designers, engineers, and scientists. Formerly a journalist, Matt has written a dozen children's books, and he enjoys cooking and baking, wine, film, reading, dinner with friends and family, and hanging out with his son.